THE PASSION OF OUR LORD JESUS CHRIST

Arranged for Proclamation by Several Ministers

In accord with the 1998

LECTIONARY FOR MASS

FOR USE IN THE DIOCESES OF THE UNITED STATES OF AMERICA

CATHOLIC BOOK PUBLISHING CORP.
NEW JERSEY

Concordat cum originali:
Reverend James P. Moroney
Executive Director, Secretariat for the Liturgy
National Conference of Catholic Bishops

The present arrangements of the four Passion narratives are taken from the *New American Bible* translation approved for use in the liturgy by the National Conference of Catholic Bishops in plenary assembly on June 20, 1992, and confirmed by decree of the Sacred Congregation of Rites, October 6, 1997 (Prot. N. 1667/97/L).

Published by authority of the Bishops' Committee on the Liturgy, National Conference of Catholic Bishops.

(T-96)

978-0-89942-096-7

Printed in the U.S.A. 26 VP 8
catholicbookpublishing.com

INTRODUCTION

The story of the Passion of the Lord is sung or proclaimed by three voices, one taking the role of Christ (✠), another that of the narrator or storyteller (N), and the last, that of the people (C), or synagogue (V). The assembly may take the part of the crowd.

The Passion is to be presented by Deacons, or, in their absence, by Priests, or in their absence too, by readers. In the last case, however, the part of Christ should be reserved for the celebrant.

For the singing of the Passion, three empty lecterns are placed on the floor of the sanctuary.

Incense and candles are not to be used.

While the Verse before the Gospel is being sung, the Deacons, carrying the book of the Passion at chest level, and accompanied by two acolytes or other ministers, bow before the celebrant and, in a low voice, ask for a blessing: **Your blessing, Father.**

The Priest responds in a low voice:

May the Lord be in your heart and on your lips,
that you may proclaim his Gospel worthily and well,
in the name of the Father, and of the Son, ✠ and of the Holy Spirit.

The Deacons respond: **Amen.**

If the readers are not Deacons, they do not ask for a blessing. At a Mass, however, at which a Bishop presides, Priests who sing or proclaim the Passion story in the absence of Deacons, ask for and receive the blessing from the Bishop.

Following this, the Deacons with the acolytes make the usual reverence and proceed to the lecterns. The Deacon who takes the role of Christ stands in the middle; to his right, whoever takes the part of the narrator and to the left, whoever takes the part of the people.

The Passion of the Lord is begun directly: **The Lord be with you** is not said, nor is the response, **Glory to you, O Lord.** When the Deacons begin to sing, they sign neither themselves nor the book.

After the announcement of the Death of the Lord, all genuflect in place and pause for a short while.

When the singing of the Passion is completed, the Deacon who took the part of the narrator says: **The Gospel of the Lord,** and all respond: **Praise to you, Lord Jesus Christ.**

The book of the Passion is not kissed by anyone. The Deacons, carrying the book, return to their chairs accompanied by the acolytes. The lecterns are removed.

Every effort should be made to proclaim the Scriptures in a clear voice and with the solemn meaning that the words of the Passion convey.

Explanation of Symbols

✠ = **Christ**

N = **Narrator**

V = **Voice**

C = **Crowd**

CONTENTS

Order of the Passion for Palm Sunday

2024 — B	2032 — A
2025 — C	2033 — B
2026 — A	2034 — C
2027 — B	2035 — A
2028 — C	2036 — B
2029 — A	2037 — C
2030 — B	2038 — A
2031 — C	2039 — B

PALM SUNDAY, PASSION "A"

THE PASSION OF OUR LORD JESUS CHRIST ACCORDING TO MATTHEW

LONGER FORM 26:14—27:66

N The Passion of our Lord Jesus Christ according to Matthew

N One of the Twelve, who was called Judas Iscariot,
went to the chief priests and said,

V *"What are you willing to give me*
if I hand him over to you?"

N They paid him thirty pieces of silver,
and from that time on he looked for an opportunity to hand him over.

On the first day of the Feast of Unleavened Bread,
the disciples approached Jesus and said,

V *"Where do you want us to prepare*
for you to eat the Passover?"

N He said,

✠ **"Go into the city to a certain man and tell him,**
'The teacher says, "My appointed time draws near;
in your house I shall celebrate the Passover with my disciples."'"

N The disciples then did as Jesus had ordered,
and prepared the Passover

When it was evening,
he reclined at table with the Twelve.
And while they were eating, he said,

✠ **"Amen, I say to you, one of you will betray me."**

N Deeply distressed at this,
they began to say to him one after another,

V *"Surely it is not I, Lord?"*

N He said in reply,

✠ **"He who has dipped his hand into the dish with me**
is the one who will betray me.
The Son of Man indeed goes, as it is written of him,
but woe to that man by whom the Son of Man is betrayed.
It would be better for that man if he had never been born."

N Then Judas, his betrayer, said in reply,

V *"Surely it is not I, Rabbi?"*

N He answered,

✠ **"You have said so."**

N While they were eating,
Jesus took bread, said the blessing,
broke it, and giving it to his disciples said,

✠ **"Take and eat; this is my body."**

N Then he took a cup, gave thanks, and gave it to them, saying,

✠ **"Drink from it, all of you,**
for this is my blood of the covenant,
which will be shed on behalf of many
for the forgiveness of sins.
I tell you, from now on I shall not drink this fruit of the vine
until the day when I drink it with you new
in the kingdom of my Father."

N Then, after singing a hymn,
they went out to the Mount of Olives.

Then Jesus said to them,

✠ **"This night all of you will have your faith in me shaken,**
for it is written:
I will strike the shepherd,
and the sheep of the flock will be dispersed;
but after I have been raised up,
I shall go before you to Galilee."

N Peter said to him in reply,

V *"Though all may have their faith in you shaken,*
mine will never be."

N Jesus said to him,

✠ **"Amen, I say to you,**
this very night before the cock crows,
you will deny me three times."

N Peter said to him,

V *"Even though I should have to die with you,*
I will not deny you."

N And all the disciples spoke likewise.

Then Jesus came with them to a place called Gethsemane,
and he said to his disciples,

✠ **"Sit here while I go over there and pray."**

N He took along Peter and the two sons of Zebedee,
and began to feel sorrow and distress.
Then he said to them,

✠ **"My soul is sorrowful even to death.**
Remain here and keep watch with me."

N He advanced a little and fell prostrate in prayer, saying,

✠ **"My Father, if it is possible,**
let this cup pass from me;
yet, not as I will, but as you will."

N When he returned to his disciples he found them asleep.
He said to Peter,

✠ **"So you could not keep watch with me for one hour?
Watch and pray that you may not undergo the test.
The spirit is willing, but the flesh is weak."**

N Withdrawing a second time, he prayed again,

✠ **"My Father, if it is not possible that this cup pass without my drinking it, your will be done!"**

N Then he returned once more and found them asleep,
for they could not keep their eyes open.
He left them and withdrew again and prayed a third time,
saying the same thing again.
Then he returned to his disciples and said to them,

✠ **"Are you still sleeping and taking your rest?
Behold, the hour is at hand
when the Son of Man is to be handed over to sinners.
Get up, let us go.
Look, my betrayer is at hand."**

N While he was still speaking,
Judas, one of the Twelve, arrived,
accompanied by a large crowd, with swords and clubs,
who had come from the chief priests and the elders of the people.
His betrayer had arranged a sign with them, saying,

V *"The man I shall kiss is the one; arrest him."*

N Immediately he went over to Jesus and said,

V *"Hail, Rabbi!"*

N and he kissed him.
Jesus answered him,

✠ **"Friend, do what you have come for."**

N Then stepping forward they laid hands on Jesus and arrested him.
And behold, one of those who accompanied Jesus
put his hand to his sword, drew it,
and struck the high priest's servant, cutting off his ear.
Then Jesus said to him,

✠ **"Put your sword back into its sheath,**
for all who take the sword will perish by the sword.
Do you think that I cannot call upon my Father
and he will not provide me at this moment
with more than twelve legions of angels?
But then how would the Scriptures be fulfilled
which say that it must come to pass in this way?"

N At that hour Jesus said to the crowds,

✠ **"Have you come out as against a robber,**
with swords and clubs to seize me?
Day after day I sat teaching in the temple area,
yet you did not arrest me.
But all this has come to pass
that the writings of the prophets may be fulfilled."

N Then all the disciples left him and fled.

Those who had arrested Jesus led him away
to Caiaphas the high priest,
where the scribes and the elders were assembled.
Peter was following him at a distance
as far as the high priest's courtyard,
and going inside he sat down with the servants to see the outcome.

The chief priests and the entire Sanhedrin
kept trying to obtain false testimony against Jesus
in order to put him to death,
but they found none,
though many false witnesses came forward.
Finally two came forward who stated,

C *"This man said, 'I can destroy the temple of God*
and within three days rebuild it.' "

N The high priest rose and addressed him,

V *"Have you no answer?*
What are these men testifying against you?"

N But Jesus was silent.
Then the high priest said to him,

V *"I order you to tell us under oath before the living God*
whether you are the Christ, the Son of God."

N Jesus said to him in reply,

✠ **"You have said so.**
But I tell you:
From now on you will see 'the Son of Man
seated at the right hand of the Power'
and 'coming on the clouds of heaven.' "

N Then the high priest tore his robes and said,

V *"He has blasphemed!*
What further need have we of witnesses?
You have now heard the blasphemy;
what is your opinion?"

N They said in reply,

C *"He deserves to die!"*

N Then they spat in his face and struck him,
while some slapped him, saying,

C *"Prophesy for us, Christ: who is it that struck you?"*

N Now Peter was sitting outside in the courtyard.
One of the maids came over to him and said,

C *"You too were with Jesus the Galilean."*

N But he denied it in front of everyone, saying,

V *"I do not know what you are talking about!"*

N As he went out to the gate, another girl saw him
and said to those who were there,

C *"This man was with Jesus the Nazorean."*

N Again he denied it with an oath,

V *"I do not know the man!"*

N A little later the bystanders came over and said to Peter,

C *"Surely you too are one of them;
even your speech gives you away."*

N At that he began to curse and to swear,

V *"I do not know the man."*

N And immediately a cock crowed.
Then Peter remembered the word that Jesus had spoken:
"Before the cock crows you will deny me three times."
He went out and began to weep bitterly.

When it was morning,
all the chief priests and the elders of the people
took counsel against Jesus to put him to death.
They bound him, led him away,
and handed him over to Pilate, the governor.

Then Judas, his betrayer, seeing that Jesus had been condemned,
deeply regretted what he had done.
He returned the thirty pieces of silver
to the chief priests and elders, saying,

V *"I have sinned in betraying innocent blood."*

N They said,

C *"What is that to us?
Look to it yourself."*

N Flinging the money into the temple,
he departed and went off and hanged himself.
The chief priests gathered up the money, but said,

C *“It is not lawful to deposit this in the temple treasury,*
for it is the price of blood.”

N After consultation, they used it to buy the potter’s field
as a burial place for foreigners.
That is why that field even today is called the Field of Blood.
Then was fulfilled what had been said through Jeremiah the prophet,
And they took the thirty pieces of silver,
the value of a man with a price on his head,
a price set by some of the Israelites,
and they paid it out for the potter’s field
just as the Lord had commanded me.

Now Jesus stood before the governor, who questioned him,

V *“Are you the king of the Jews?”*

N Jesus said,

✠ **“You say so.”**

N And when he was accused by the chief priests and elders,
he made no answer.
Then Pilate said to him,

V *“Do you not hear how many things they are testifying against you?”*

N But he did not answer him one word,
so that the governor was greatly amazed.

Now on the occasion of the feast
the governor was accustomed to release to the crowd
one prisoner whom they wished.
And at that time they had a notorious prisoner called Barabbas.
So when they had assembled, Pilate said to them,

V *"Which one do you want me to release to you,*
Barabbas, or Jesus called Christ?"

N For he knew that it was out of envy
that they had handed him over.
While he was still seated on the bench,
his wife sent him a message,
"Have nothing to do with that righteous man.
I suffered much in a dream today because of him."

The chief priests and the elders persuaded the crowds
to ask for Barabbas but to destroy Jesus.
The governor said to them in reply,

V *"Which of the two do you want me to release to you?"*

N They answered,

C *"Barabbas!"*

N Pilate said to them,

V *"Then what shall I do with Jesus called Christ?"*

N They all said,

C *"Let him be crucified!"*

N But he said,

V *"Why? What evil has he done?"*

N They only shouted the louder,

C *"Let him be crucified!"*

N When Pilate saw that he was not succeeding at all,
but that a riot was breaking out instead,
he took water and washed his hands in the sight of the crowd, saying,

V *"I am innocent of this man's blood.*
Look to it yourselves."

N And the whole people said in reply,

C *"His blood be upon us and upon our children."*

N Then he released Barabbas to them,
but after he had Jesus scourged,
he handed him over to be crucified.

Then the soldiers of the governor took Jesus inside the praetorium
and gathered the whole cohort around him.
They stripped off his clothes
and threw a scarlet military cloak about him.
Weaving a crown out of thorns, they placed it on his head,
and a reed in his right hand.
And kneeling before him, they mocked him, saying,

C *"Hail, King of the Jews!"*

N They spat upon him and took the reed
and kept striking him on the head.
And when they had mocked him,
they stripped him of the cloak,
dressed him in his own clothes,
and led him off to crucify him.

As they were going out, they met a Cyrenian named Simon;
this man they pressed into service
to carry his cross.

And when they came to a place called Golgotha
— which means Place of the Skull —,
they gave Jesus wine to drink mixed with gall.
But when he had tasted it, he refused to drink.
After they had crucified him,
they divided his garments by casting lots;
then they sat down and kept watch over him there.
And they placed over his head the written charge against him:
This is Jesus, the King of the Jews.

Two revolutionaries were crucified with him,
one on his right and the other on his left.
Those passing by reviled him, shaking their heads and saying,

C *"You who would destroy the temple and rebuild it in three days,*
save yourself, if you are the Son of God,
and come down from the cross!"

N Likewise the chief priests with the scribes and elders mocked him and said,

C *"He saved others; he cannot save himself.*
So he is the king of Israel!
Let him come down from the cross now,
and we will believe in him.
He trusted in God;
let him deliver him now if he wants him.
For he said, 'I am the Son of God.' "

N The revolutionaries who were crucified with him
also kept abusing him in the same way.

From noon onward, darkness came over the whole land
until three in the afternoon.
And about three o'clock Jesus cried out in a loud voice,

✠ **"Eli, Eli, lema sabachthani?"**

N which means,

✠ **"My God, my God, why have you forsaken me?"**

N Some of the bystanders who heard it said,

C *"This one is calling for Elijah."*

N Immediately one of them ran to get a sponge;
he soaked it in wine, and putting it on a reed,
gave it to him to drink.
But the rest said,

C *"Wait, let us see if Elijah comes to save him."*

N But Jesus cried out again in a loud voice,
and gave up his spirit.

Here all kneel and pause for a short time.

N And behold, the veil of the sanctuary
was torn in two from top to bottom.
The earth quaked, rocks were split, tombs were opened,
and the bodies of many saints who had fallen asleep were raised.
And coming forth from their tombs after his resurrection,
they entered the holy city and appeared to many.
The centurion and the men with him who were keeping watch over Jesus
feared greatly when they saw the earthquake
and all that was happening, and they said,

C *"Truly, this was the Son of God!"*

N There were many women there, looking on from a distance,
who had followed Jesus from Galilee, ministering to him.
Among them were Mary Magdalene and Mary the mother of James and Joseph,
and the mother of the sons of Zebedee.

When it was evening,
there came a rich man from Arimathea named Joseph,
who was himself a disciple of Jesus.
He went to Pilate and asked for the body of Jesus;
then Pilate ordered it to be handed over.
Taking the body, Joseph wrapped it in clean linen
and laid it in his new tomb that he had hewn in the rock.
Then he rolled a huge stone across the entrance to the tomb and departed.
But Mary Magdalene and the other Mary
remained sitting there, facing the tomb.
The next day, the one following the day of preparation,
the chief priests and the Pharisees
gathered before Pilate and said,

C *"Sir, we remember that this impostor while still alive said,*
'After three days I will be raised up.'
Give orders, then, that the grave be secured until the third day,
lest his disciples come and steal him and say to the people,
'He has been raised from the dead.'
This last imposture would be worse than the first."

N Pilate said to them,

V *"The guard is yours;*
go, secure it as best you can."

N So they went and secured the tomb
by fixing a seal to the stone and setting the guard.

The Gospel of the Lord.

PALM SUNDAY, PASSION "A"

THE PASSION OF OUR LORD JESUS CHRIST ACCORDING TO MATTHEW

SHORTER FORM 27:11-54

N The Passion of our Lord Jesus Christ according to Matthew

N Jesus stood before the governor, Pontius Pilate, who questioned him,

V *"Are you the king of the Jews?"*

N Jesus said,

✠ **"You say so."**

N And when he was accused by the chief priests and elders,
he made no answer.
Then Pilate said to him,

V *"Do you not hear how many things they are testifying against you?"*

N But he did not answer him one word,
so that the governor was greatly amazed.

Now on the occasion of the feast
the governor was accustomed to release to the crowd
one prisoner whom they wished.
And at that time they had a notorious prisoner called Barabbas.
So when they had assembled, Pilate said to them,

V *"Which one do you want me to release to you,*
Barabbas, or Jesus called Christ?"

N For he knew that it was out of envy
that they had handed him over.
While he was still seated on the bench,
his wife sent him a message,
"Have nothing to do with that righteous man.
I suffered much in a dream today because of him."

The chief priests and the elders persuaded the crowds
to ask for Barabbas but to destroy Jesus.
The governor said to them in reply,

V *"Which of the two do you want me to release to you?"*

N They answered,

C *"Barabbas!"*

N Pilate said to them,

V *"Then what shall I do with Jesus called Christ?"*

N They all said,

C *"Let him be crucified!"*

N But he said,

V *"Why? What evil has he done?"*

N They only shouted the louder,

C *"Let him be crucified!"*

N When Pilate saw that he was not succeeding at all,
but that a riot was breaking out instead,
he took water and washed his hands in the sight of the crowd, saying,

V *"I am innocent of this man's blood.*
Look to it yourselves."

N And the whole people said in reply,

C *"His blood be upon us and upon our children."*

N Then he released Barabbas to them,
but after he had Jesus scourged,
he handed him over to be crucified.

Then the soldiers of the governor took Jesus inside the praetorium
and gathered the whole cohort around him.

They stripped off his clothes
and threw a scarlet military cloak about him.
Weaving a crown out of thorns, they placed it on his head,
and a reed in his right hand.
And kneeling before him, they mocked him, saying,

C *"Hail, King of the Jews!"*

N They spat upon him and took the reed
and kept striking him on the head.
And when they had mocked him,
they stripped him of the cloak,
dressed him in his own clothes,
and led him off to crucify him.

As they were going out, they met a Cyrenian named Simon;
this man they pressed into service
to carry his cross.

And when they came to a place called Golgotha
— which means Place of the Skull —,
they gave Jesus wine to drink mixed with gall.
But when he had tasted it, he refused to drink.
After they had crucified him,
they divided his garments by casting lots;
then they sat down and kept watch over him there.
And they placed over his head the written charge against him:
This is Jesus, the King of the Jews.
Two revolutionaries were crucified with him,
one on his right and the other on his left.
Those passing by reviled him, shaking their heads and saying,

C *"You who would destroy the temple and rebuild it in three days,*
save yourself, if you are the Son of God,
and come down from the cross!"

N Likewise the chief priests with the scribes and elders mocked him and said,

C *"He saved others; he cannot save himself.*
So he is the king of Israel!
Let him come down from the cross now,
and we will believe in him.
He trusted in God;
let him deliver him now if he wants him.
For he said, 'I am the Son of God.' "

N The revolutionaries who were crucified with him
also kept abusing him in the same way.

From noon onward, darkness came over the whole land
until three in the afternoon.
And about three o'clock Jesus cried out in a loud voice,

✠ **"Eli, Eli, lema sabachthani?"**

N which means,

✠ **"My God, my God, why have you forsaken me?"**

N Some of the bystanders who heard it said,

C *"This one is calling for Elijah."*

N Immediately one of them ran to get a sponge;
he soaked it in wine, and putting it on a reed,
gave it to him to drink.
But the rest said,

C *"Wait, let us see if Elijah comes to save him."*

N But Jesus cried out again in a loud voice,
and gave up his spirit.

Here all kneel and pause for a short time.

N And behold, the veil of the sanctuary
was torn in two from top to bottom.

The earth quaked, rocks were split, tombs were opened,
and the bodies of many saints who had fallen asleep were raised.
And coming forth from their tombs after his resurrection,
they entered the holy city and appeared to many.
The centurion and the men with him who were keeping watch over Jesus
feared greatly when they saw the earthquake
and all that was happening, and they said,

C *"Truly, this was the Son of God!"*

The Gospel of the Lord.

PALM SUNDAY, PASSION "B"

THE PASSION OF OUR LORD JESUS CHRIST ACCORDING TO MARK

LONGER FORM 14:1—15:47

N The Passion of our Lord Jesus Christ according to Mark

N The Passover and the Feast of Unleavened Bread
were to take place in two days' time.
So the chief priests and the scribes were seeking a way
to arrest him by treachery and put him to death.
They said,

C *"Not during the festival,*
for fear that there may be a riot among the people."

N When he was in Bethany reclining at table
in the house of Simon the leper,
a woman came with an alabaster jar of perfumed oil,
costly genuine spikenard.
She broke the alabaster jar and poured it on his head.
There were some who were indignant.

C *"Why has there been this waste of perfumed oil?*
It could have been sold for more than three hundred days' wages
and the money given to the poor."

N They were infuriated with her.
Jesus said,

✠ **"Let her alone.**
Why do you make trouble for her?
She has done a good thing for me.
The poor you will always have with you,
and whenever you wish you can do good to them,
but you will not always have me.
She has done what she could.
She has anticipated anointing my body for burial.

Amen, I say to you,
wherever the gospel is proclaimed to the whole world,
what she has done will be told in memory of her."

N Then Judas Iscariot, one of the Twelve,
went off to the chief priests to hand him over to them.
When they heard him they were pleased and promised to pay him money.
Then he looked for an opportunity to hand him over.

On the first day of the Feast of Unleavened Bread,
when they sacrificed the Passover lamb,
his disciples said to him,

C *"Where do you want us to go*
and prepare for you to eat the Passover?"

N He sent two of his disciples and said to them,

✠ **"Go into the city and a man will meet you,**
carrying a jar of water.
Follow him.
Wherever he enters, say to the master of the house,
'The Teacher says, "Where is my guest room
where I may eat the Passover with my disciples?" '
Then he will show you a large upper room furnished and ready.
Make the preparations for us there."

N The disciples then went off, entered the city,
and found it just as he had told them;
and they prepared the Passover.

When it was evening, he came with the Twelve.
And as they reclined at table and were eating, Jesus said,

✠ **"Amen, I say to you, one of you will betray me,**
one who is eating with me."

N They began to be distressed and to say to him, one by one,

V *"Surely it is not I?"*

N He said to them,

✠ **"One of the Twelve, the one who dips with me into the dish.**
For the Son of Man indeed goes, as it is written of him,
but woe to that man by whom the Son of Man is betrayed.
It would be better for that man if he had never been born."

N While they were eating,
he took bread, said the blessing,
broke it, and gave it to them, and said,

✠ **"Take it; this is my body."**

N Then he took a cup, gave thanks, and gave it to them,
and they all drank from it.
He said to them,

✠ **"This is my blood of the covenant,**
which will be shed for many.
Amen, I say to you,
I shall not drink again the fruit of the vine
until the day when I drink it new in the kingdom of God."

N Then, after singing a hymn,
they went out to the Mount of Olives.

Then Jesus said to them,

✠ **"All of you will have your faith shaken, for it is written:**
I will strike the shepherd,
and the sheep will be dispersed.
But after I have been raised up,
I shall go before you to Galilee."

N Peter said to him,

V *"Even though all should have their faith shaken,*
mine will not be."

N Then Jesus said to him,

✠ **"Amen, I say to you,**
this very night before the cock crows twice
you will deny me three times."

N But he vehemently replied,

V *"Even though I should have to die with you,*
I will not deny you."

N And they all spoke similarly.

Then they came to a place named Gethsemane,
and he said to his disciples,

✠ **"Sit here while I pray."**

N He took with him Peter, James, and John,
and began to be troubled and distressed.
Then he said to them,

✠ **"My soul is sorrowful even to death.**
Remain here and keep watch."

N He advanced a little and fell to the ground and prayed
that if it were possible the hour might pass by him;
he said,

✠ **"Abba, Father, all things are possible to you.**
Take this cup away from me,
but not what I will but what you will."

N When he returned he found them asleep.
He said to Peter,

✠ **"Simon, are you asleep?**
Could you not keep watch for one hour?
Watch and pray that you may not undergo the test.
The spirit is willing but the flesh is weak."

N Withdrawing again, he prayed, saying the same thing.
Then he returned once more and found them asleep,
for they could not keep their eyes open
and did not know what to answer him.
He returned a third time and said to them,

✠ **"Are you still sleeping and taking your rest?
It is enough. The hour has come.
Behold, the Son of Man is to be handed over to sinners.
Get up, let us go.
See, my betrayer is at hand."**

N Then, while he was still speaking,
Judas, one of the Twelve, arrived,
accompanied by a crowd with swords and clubs
who had come from the chief priests,
the scribes, and the elders.
His betrayer had arranged a signal with them, saying,

V *"The man I shall kiss is the one;
arrest him and lead him away securely."*

N He came and immediately went over to him and said,

V *"Rabbi."*

N And he kissed him.
At this they laid hands on him and arrested him.
One of the bystanders drew his sword,
struck the high priest's servant, and cut off his ear.
Jesus said to them in reply,

✠ **"Have you come out as against a robber,
with swords and clubs, to seize me?
Day after day I was with you teaching in the temple area,
yet you did not arrest me;
but that the Scriptures may be fulfilled."**

N And they all left him and fled.
Now a young man followed him
wearing nothing but a linen cloth about his body.
They seized him,
but he left the cloth behind and ran off naked.

They led Jesus away to the high priest,
and all the chief priests and the elders and the scribes
came together.

Peter followed him at a distance into the high priest's courtyard
and was seated with the guards, warming himself at the fire.
The chief priests and the entire Sanhedrin
kept trying to obtain testimony against Jesus
in order to put him to death, but they found none.
Many gave false witness against him,
but their testimony did not agree.
Some took the stand and testified falsely against him, alleging,

C *"We heard him say,*
'I will destroy this temple made with hands
and within three days I will build another
not made with hands.' "

N Even so their testimony did not agree.
The high priest rose before the assembly and questioned Jesus, saying,

V *"Have you no answer?*
What are these men testifying against you?"

N But he was silent and answered nothing.
Again the high priest asked him and said to him,

V *"Are you the Christ, the son of the Blessed One?"*

N Then Jesus answered,

✠ **"I am;**
and 'you will see the Son of Man
seated at the right hand of the Power
and coming with the clouds of heaven.' "

N At that the high priest tore his garments and said,

V *"What further need have we of witnesses?*
You have heard the blasphemy.
What do you think?"

N They all condemned him as deserving to die.
Some began to spit on him.
They blindfolded him and struck him and said to him,

C *"Prophesy!"*

N And the guards greeted him with blows.

While Peter was below in the courtyard,
one of the high priest's maids came along.
Seeing Peter warming himself,
she looked intently at him and said,

C *"You too were with the Nazorean, Jesus."*

N But he denied it saying,

V *"I neither know nor understand what you are talking about."*

N So he went out into the outer court.
Then the cock crowed.
The maid saw him and began again to say to the bystanders,

C *"This man is one of them."*

N Once again he denied it.
A little later the bystanders said to Peter once more,

C *"Surely you are one of them; for you too are a Galilean."*

N He began to curse and to swear,

V *"I do not know this man about whom you are talking."*

N And immediately a cock crowed a second time.
Then Peter remembered the word that Jesus had said to him,
"Before the cock crows twice you will deny me three times."
He broke down and wept.

As soon as morning came,
the chief priests with the elders and the scribes,

that is, the whole Sanhedrin, held a council.
They bound Jesus, led him away, and handed him over to Pilate.
Pilate questioned him,

V *"Are you the king of the Jews?"*

N He said to him in reply,

✠ **"You say so."**

N The chief priests accused him of many things.
Again Pilate questioned him,

V *"Have you no answer?*
See how many things they accuse you of."

N Jesus gave him no further answer, so that Pilate was amazed.

Now on the occasion of the feast he used to release to them one prisoner whom they requested.
A man called Barabbas was then in prison
along with the rebels who had committed murder in a rebellion.
The crowd came forward and began to ask him
to do for them as he was accustomed.
Pilate answered,

V *"Do you want me to release to you the king of the Jews?"*

N For he knew that it was out of envy
that the chief priests had handed him over.
But the chief priests stirred up the crowd
to have him release Barabbas for them instead.
Pilate again said to them in reply,

V *"Then what do you want me to do*
with the man you call the king of the Jews?"

N They shouted again,

C *"Crucify him."*

N Pilate said to them,

V *"Why? What evil has he done?"*

N They only shouted the louder,

C *"Crucify him."*

N So Pilate, wishing to satisfy the crowd,
released Barabbas to them and, after he had Jesus scourged,
handed him over to be crucified.

The soldiers led him away inside the palace,
that is, the praetorium, and assembled the whole cohort.
They clothed him in purple and,
weaving a crown of thorns, placed it on him.
They began to salute him with,

C *"Hail, King of the Jews!"*

N and kept striking his head with a reed and spitting upon him.
They knelt before him in homage.
And when they had mocked him,
they stripped him of the purple cloak,
dressed him in his own clothes,
and led him out to crucify him.

They pressed into service a passer-by, Simon,
a Cyrenian, who was coming in from the country,
the father of Alexander and Rufus,
to carry his cross.

They brought him to the place of Golgotha
—which is translated Place of the Skull—.
They gave him wine drugged with myrrh,
but he did not take it.
Then they crucified him and divided his garments
by casting lots for them to see what each should take.

It was nine o'clock in the morning when they crucified him.
The inscription of the charge against him read,
"The King of the Jews."
With him they crucified two revolutionaries,
one on his right and one on his left.
Those passing by reviled him,
shaking their heads and saying,

C *"Aha! You who would destroy the temple*
and rebuild it in three days,
save yourself by coming down from the cross."

N Likewise the chief priests, with the scribes,
mocked him among themselves and said,

C *"He saved others; he cannot save himself.*
Let the Christ, the King of Israel,
come down now from the cross
that we may see and believe."

N Those who were crucified with him also kept abusing him.

At noon darkness came over the whole land
until three in the afternoon.
And at three o'clock Jesus cried out in a loud voice,

✠ ***"Eloi, Eloi, lema sabachthani?"***

N which is translated,

✠ **"My God, my God, why have you forsaken me?"**

N Some of the bystanders who heard it said,

C *"Look, he is calling Elijah."*

N One of them ran, soaked a sponge with wine, put it on a reed
and gave it to him to drink, saying,

V *"Wait, let us see if Elijah comes to take him down."*

N Jesus gave a loud cry and breathed his last.

Here all kneel and pause for a short time.

N The veil of the sanctuary was torn in two from top to bottom.
When the centurion who stood facing him
saw how he breathed his last he said,

V *"Truly this man was the Son of God!"*

N There were also women looking on from a distance.
Among them were Mary Magdalene,
Mary the mother of the younger James and of Joses, and Salome.
These women had followed him when he was in Galilee
and ministered to him.
There were also many other women
who had come up with him to Jerusalem.

When it was already evening,
since it was the day of preparation,
the day before the sabbath, Joseph of Arimathea,
a distinguished member of the council,
who was himself awaiting the kingdom of God,
came and courageously went to Pilate
and asked for the body of Jesus.
Pilate was amazed that he was already dead.
He summoned the centurion
and asked him if Jesus had already died.
And when he learned of it from the centurion,
he gave the body to Joseph.
Having bought a linen cloth, he took him down,
wrapped him in the linen cloth,
and laid him in a tomb that had been hewn out of the rock.
Then he rolled a stone against the entrance to the tomb.
Mary Magdalene and Mary the mother of Joses
watched where he was laid.

The Gospel of the Lord.

PALM SUNDAY, PASSION "B"

THE PASSION OF OUR LORD JESUS CHRIST ACCORDING TO MARK

SHORTER FORM 15:1-39

N The Passion of our Lord Jesus Christ according to Mark

N As soon as morning came,
the chief priests with the elders and the scribes,
that is, the whole Sanhedrin, held a council.
They bound Jesus, led him away, and handed him over to Pilate.
Pilate questioned him,

V *"Are you the king of the Jews?"*

N He said to him in reply,

✠ **"You say so."**

N The chief priests accused him of many things.
Again Pilate questioned him,

V *"Have you no answer?*
See how many things they accuse you of."

N Jesus gave him no further answer, so that Pilate was amazed.

Now on the occasion of the feast he used to release to them
one prisoner whom they requested.
A man called Barabbas was then in prison
along with the rebels who had committed murder in a rebellion.
The crowd came forward and began to ask him
to do for them as he was accustomed.
Pilate answered,

V *"Do you want me to release to you the king of the Jews?"*

N For he knew that it was out of envy
that the chief priests had handed him over.
But the chief priests stirred up the crowd
to have him release Barabbas for them instead.
Pilate again said to them in reply,

V *"Then what do you want me to do
with the man you call the king of the Jews?"*

N They shouted again,

C *"Crucify him."*

N Pilate said to them,

V *"Why? What evil has he done?"*

N They only shouted the louder,

C *"Crucify him."*

N So Pilate, wishing to satisfy the crowd,
released Barabbas to them and, after he had Jesus scourged,
handed him over to be crucified.

The soldiers led him away inside the palace,
that is, the praetorium, and assembled the whole cohort.
They clothed him in purple and,
weaving a crown of thorns, placed it on him.
They began to salute him with,

C *"Hail, King of the Jews!"*

N and kept striking his head with a reed and spitting upon him.
They knelt before him in homage.
And when they had mocked him,
they stripped him of the purple cloak,
dressed him in his own clothes,
and led him out to crucify him.

They pressed into service a passer-by, Simon,
a Cyrenian, who was coming in from the country,
the father of Alexander and Rufus,
to carry his cross.

They brought him to the place of Golgotha
—which is translated Place of the Skull—.
They gave him wine drugged with myrrh,
but he did not take it.
Then they crucified him and divided his garments
by casting lots for them to see what each should take.
It was nine o'clock in the morning when they crucified him.
The inscription of the charge against him read,
"The King of the Jews."
With him they crucified two revolutionaries,
one on his right and one on his left.
Those passing by reviled him,
shaking their heads and saying,

C *"Aha! You who would destroy the temple*
and rebuild it in three days,
save yourself by coming down from the cross."

N Likewise the chief priests, with the scribes,
mocked him among themselves and said,

C *"He saved others; he cannot save himself.*
Let the Christ, the King of Israel,
come down now from the cross
that we may see and believe."

N Those who were crucified with him also kept abusing him.

At noon darkness came over the whole land
until three in the afternoon.
And at three o'clock Jesus cried out in a loud voice,

✠ ***"Eloi, Eloi, lema sabachthani?"***

N which is translated,

✠ **"My God, my God, why have you forsaken me?"**

N Some of the bystanders who heard it said,

C *"Look, he is calling Elijah."*

N One of them ran, soaked a sponge with wine, put it on a reed
and gave it to him to drink, saying,

V *"Wait, let us see if Elijah comes to take him down."*

N Jesus gave a loud cry and breathed his last.

Here all kneel and pause for a short time.

N The veil of the sanctuary was torn in two from top to bottom.
When the centurion who stood facing him
saw how he breathed his last he said,

V *"Truly this man was the Son of God!"*

The Gospel of the Lord.

PALM SUNDAY, PASSION "C"

THE PASSION OF OUR LORD JESUS CHRIST ACCORDING TO LUKE

LONGER FORM 22:14—23:56

N The Passion of our Lord Jesus Christ according to Luke

N When the hour came,
Jesus took his place at table with the apostles.
He said to them,

✠ **"I have eagerly desired to eat this Passover with you before I suffer,**
for, I tell you, I shall not eat it again
until there is fulfillment in the kingdom of God."

N Then he took a cup, gave thanks, and said,

✠ **"Take this and share it among yourselves;**
for I tell you that from this time on
I shall not drink of the fruit of the vine
until the kingdom of God comes."

N Then he took the bread, said the blessing,
broke it, and gave it to them, saying,

✠ **"This is my body, which will be given for you;**
do this in memory of me."

N And likewise the cup after they had eaten, saying,

✠ **"This cup is the new covenant in my blood,**
which will be shed for you.

"And yet behold, the hand of the one who is to betray me is with me on the table;
for the Son of Man indeed goes as it has been determined;
but woe to that man by whom he is betrayed."

N And they began to debate among themselves
who among them would do such a deed.
Then an argument broke out among them
about which of them should be regarded as the greatest.
He said to them,

✠ **"The kings of the Gentiles lord it over them**
and those in authority over them are addressed as 'Benefactors';
but among you it shall not be so.
Rather, let the greatest among you be as the youngest,
and the leader as the servant.
For who is greater:
the one seated at table or the one who serves?
Is it not the one seated at table?
I am among you as the one who serves.
It is you who have stood by me in my trials;
and I confer a kingdom on you,
just as my Father has conferred one on me,
that you may eat and drink at my table in my kingdom;
and you will sit on thrones
judging the twelve tribes of Israel.

"Simon, Simon, behold Satan has demanded
to sift all of you like wheat,
but I have prayed that your own faith may not fail;
and once you have turned back,
you must strengthen your brothers."

N He said to him,

V *"Lord, I am prepared to go to prison and to die with you."*

N But he replied,

✠ **"I tell you, Peter, before the cock crows this day,**
you will deny three times that you know me."

N He said to them,

✠ **"When I sent you forth without a money bag or a sack or sandals,**
were you in need of anything?"

C "No, nothing,"

N they replied.
He said to them,

✠ **"But now one who has a money bag should take it, and likewise a sack,**
and one who does not have a sword
should sell his cloak and buy one.
For I tell you that this Scripture must be fulfilled in me,
namely, *He was counted among the wicked;*
and indeed what is written about me is coming to fulfillment."

N Then they said,

C *"Lord, look, there are two swords here."*

N But he replied,

✠ **"It is enough!"**

N Then going out, he went, as was his custom, to the Mount of Olives,
and the disciples followed him.
When he arrived at the place he said to them,

✠ **"Pray that you may not undergo the test."**

N After withdrawing about a stone's throw from them and kneeling,
he prayed, saying,

✠ **"Father, if you are willing,**
take this cup away from me;
still, not my will but yours be done."

N And to strengthen him an angel from heaven appeared to him.
He was in such agony and he prayed so fervently
that his sweat became like drops of blood
falling on the ground.
When he rose from prayer and returned to his disciples,
he found them sleeping from grief.
He said to them,

✠ **"Why are you sleeping?**
Get up and pray that you may not undergo the test."

N While he was still speaking, a crowd approached
and in front was one of the Twelve, a man named Judas.
He went up to Jesus to kiss him.
Jesus said to him,

✠ **"Judas, are you betraying the Son of Man with a kiss?"**

N His disciples realized what was about to happen, and they asked,

C *"Lord, shall we strike with a sword?"*

N And one of them struck the high priest's servant
and cut off his right ear.
But Jesus said in reply,

✠ **"Stop, no more of this!"**

N Then he touched the servant's ear and healed him.
And Jesus said to the chief priests and temple guards
and elders who had come for him,

✠ **"Have you come out as against a robber, with swords and clubs?**
Day after day I was with you in the temple area,
and you did not seize me;
but this is your hour, the time for the power of darkness."

N After arresting him they led him away
and took him into the house of the high priest;
Peter was following at a distance.
They lit a fire in the middle of the courtyard and sat around it,
and Peter sat down with them.
When a maid saw him seated in the light,
she looked intently at him and said,

C *"This man too was with him."*

N But he denied it saying,

V *"Woman, I do not know him."*

N A short while later someone else saw him and said,

C *"You too are one of them";*

N but Peter answered,

V *"My friend, I am not."*

N About an hour later, still another insisted,

C *"Assuredly, this man too was with him,*
for he also is a Galilean."

N But Peter said,

V *"My friend, I do not know what you are talking about."*

N Just as he was saying this, the cock crowed,
and the Lord turned and looked at Peter;
and Peter remembered the word of the Lord,
how he had said to him,
"Before the cock crows today, you will deny me three times."
He went out and began to weep bitterly.

The men who held Jesus in custody were ridiculing and beating him.
They blindfolded him and questioned him, saying,

C *"Prophesy! Who is it that struck you?"*

N And they reviled him in saying many other things against him.

When day came the council of elders of the people met,
both chief priests and scribes,
and they brought him before their Sanhedrin.
They said,

C *"If you are the Christ, tell us,"*

N but he replied to them,

✠ **"If I tell you, you will not believe,**
and if I question, you will not respond.
But from this time on the Son of Man will be seated
at the right hand of the power of God."

N They all asked,

C *"Are you then the Son of God?"*

N He replied to them,

✠ **"You say that I am."**

N Then they said,

C *"What further need have we for testimony?*
We have heard it from his own mouth."

N Then the whole assembly of them arose and brought him before Pilate.
They brought charges against him, saying,

C *"We found this man misleading our people;*
he opposes the payment of taxes to Caesar
and maintains that he is the Christ, a king."

N Pilate asked him,

V *"Are you the king of the Jews?"*

N He said to him in reply,

✠ **"You say so."**

N Pilate then addressed the chief priests and the crowds,

V *"I find this man not guilty."*

N But they were adamant and said,

C *"He is inciting the people with his teaching throughout all Judea,*
from Galilee where he began even to here."

N On hearing this Pilate asked if the man was a Galilean;
and upon learning that he was under Herod's jurisdiction,
he sent him to Herod who was in Jerusalem at that time.
Herod was very glad to see Jesus;
he had been wanting to see him for a long time,
for he had heard about him
and had been hoping to see him perform some sign.
He questioned him at length,
but he gave him no answer.
The chief priests and scribes, meanwhile,
stood by accusing him harshly.
Herod and his soldiers treated him contemptuously and mocked him,
and after clothing him in resplendent garb,
he sent him back to Pilate.
Herod and Pilate became friends that very day,
even though they had been enemies formerly.
Pilate then summoned the chief priests, the rulers, and the people
and said to them,

V *"You brought this man to me*
and accused him of inciting the people to revolt.
I have conducted my investigation in your presence
and have not found this man guilty
of the charges you have brought against him,
nor did Herod, for he sent him back to us.
So no capital crime has been committed by him.
Therefore I shall have him flogged and then release him."

N But all together they shouted out,

C *"Away with this man!*
Release Barabbas to us."

N —Now Barabbas had been imprisoned for a rebellion
that had taken place in the city and for murder.—
Again Pilate addressed them, still wishing to release Jesus,
but they continued their shouting,

C *"Crucify him! Crucify him!"*

N Pilate addressed them a third time,

V *"What evil has this man done?*
I found him guilty of no capital crime.
Therefore I shall have him flogged and then release him."

N With loud shouts, however,
they persisted in calling for his crucifixion,
and their voices prevailed.
The verdict of Pilate was that their demand should be granted.
So he released the man who had been imprisoned
for rebellion and murder, for whom they asked,
and he handed Jesus over to them to deal with as they wished.

As they led him away
they took hold of a certain Simon, a Cyrenian,
who was coming in from the country;
and after laying the cross on him,
they made him carry it behind Jesus.
A large crowd of people followed Jesus,
including many women who mourned and lamented him.
Jesus turned to them and said,

✠ **"Daughters of Jerusalem, do not weep for me;**
weep instead for yourselves and for your children,
for indeed, the days are coming when people will say,
'Blessed are the barren,
the wombs that never bore
and the breasts that never nursed.'
At that time people will say to the mountains,
'Fall upon us!'
and to the hills, 'Cover us!'
for if these things are done when the wood is green
what will happen when it is dry?"

N Now two others, both criminals,
were led away with him to be executed.

When they came to the place called the Skull,
they crucified him and the criminals there,
one on his right, the other on his left.
Then Jesus said,

✠ **"Father, forgive them, they know not what they do."**

N They divided his garments by casting lots.
The people stood by and watched;
the rulers, meanwhile, sneered at him and said,

C *"He saved others, let him save himself*
if he is the chosen one, the Christ of God."

N Even the soldiers jeered at him.
As they approached to offer him wine they called out,

C *"If you are King of the Jews, save yourself."*

N Above him there was an inscription that read,
"This is the King of the Jews."

Now one of the criminals hanging there reviled Jesus, saying,

V *"Are you not the Christ?*
Save yourself and us."

N The other, however, rebuking him, said in reply,

V *"Have you no fear of God,*
for you are subject to the same condemnation?
And indeed, we have been condemned justly,
for the sentence we received corresponds to our crimes,
but this man has done nothing criminal."

N Then he said,

V *"Jesus, remember me when you come into your kingdom."*

N He replied to him,

✠ **"Amen, I say to you,**
today you will be with me in Paradise."

N It was now about noon and darkness came over the whole land
until three in the afternoon
because of an eclipse of the sun.
Then the veil of the temple was torn down the middle.
Jesus cried out in a loud voice,

✠ **"Father, into your hands I commend my spirit";**

N and when he had said this he breathed his last.

Here all kneel and pause for a short time.

N The centurion who witnessed what had happened glorified God and said,

V *"This man was innocent beyond doubt."*

N When all the people who had gathered for this spectacle saw what had happened,
they returned home beating their breasts;
but all his acquaintances stood at a distance,
including the women who had followed him from Galilee
and saw these events.

Now there was a virtuous and righteous man named Joseph who,
though he was a member of the council,
had not consented to their plan of action.
He came from the Jewish town of Arimathea
and was awaiting the kingdom of God.
He went to Pilate and asked for the body of Jesus.
After he had taken the body down,
he wrapped it in a linen cloth
and laid him in a rock-hewn tomb
in which no one had yet been buried.
It was the day of preparation,
and the sabbath was about to begin.
The women who had come from Galilee with him followed behind,
and when they had seen the tomb
and the way in which his body was laid in it,
they returned and prepared spices and perfumed oils.
Then they rested on the sabbath according to the commandment.

The Gospel of the Lord.

PALM SUNDAY, PASSION "C"

THE PASSION OF OUR LORD JESUS CHRIST ACCORDING TO LUKE

SHORTER FORM 23:1-49

N The Passion of our Lord Jesus Christ according to Luke

N The elders of the people, chief priests and scribes,
arose and brought Jesus before Pilate.
They brought charges against him, saying,

C *"We found this man misleading our people;*
he opposes the payment of taxes to Caesar
and maintains that he is the Christ, a king."

N Pilate asked him,

V *"Are you the king of the Jews?"*

N He said to him in reply,

✠ **"You say so."**

N Pilate then addressed the chief priests and the crowds,

V *"I find this man not guilty."*

N But they were adamant and said,

C *"He is inciting the people with his teaching throughout all Judea,*
from Galilee where he began even to here."

N On hearing this Pilate asked if the man was a Galilean;
and upon learning that he was under Herod's jurisdiction,
he sent him to Herod who was in Jerusalem at that time.
Herod was very glad to see Jesus;
he had been wanting to see him for a long time,
for he had heard about him
and had been hoping to see him perform some sign.
He questioned him at length,
but he gave him no answer.

The chief priests and scribes, meanwhile,
stood by accusing him harshly.
Herod and his soldiers treated him contemptuously and mocked him,
and after clothing him in resplendent garb,
he sent him back to Pilate.
Herod and Pilate became friends that very day,
even though they had been enemies formerly.
Pilate then summoned the chief priests, the rulers, and the people
and said to them,

V *"You brought this man to me*
and accused him of inciting the people to revolt.
I have conducted my investigation in your presence
and have not found this man guilty
of the charges you have brought against him,
nor did Herod, for he sent him back to us.
So no capital crime has been committed by him.
Therefore I shall have him flogged and then release him."

N But all together they shouted out,

C *"Away with this man!*
Release Barabbas to us."

N —Now Barabbas had been imprisoned for a rebellion
that had taken place in the city and for murder.—
Again Pilate addressed them, still wishing to release Jesus,
but they continued their shouting,

C *"Crucify him! Crucify him!"*

N Pilate addressed them a third time,

V *"What evil has this man done?*
I found him guilty of no capital crime.
Therefore I shall have him flogged and then release him."

N With loud shouts, however,
they persisted in calling for his crucifixion,
and their voices prevailed.
The verdict of Pilate was that their demand should be granted.
So he released the man who had been imprisoned
for rebellion and murder, for whom they asked,
and he handed Jesus over to them to deal with as they wished.

As they led him away
they took hold of a certain Simon, a Cyrenian,
who was coming in from the country;
and after laying the cross on him,
they made him carry it behind Jesus.
A large crowd of people followed Jesus,
including many women who mourned and lamented him.
Jesus turned to them and said,

✠ **"Daughters of Jerusalem, do not weep for me;**
weep instead for yourselves and for your children,
for indeed, the days are coming when people will say,
'Blessed are the barren,
the wombs that never bore
and the breasts that never nursed.'
At that time people will say to the mountains,
'Fall upon us!'
and to the hills, 'Cover us!'
for if these things are done when the wood is green
what will happen when it is dry?"

N Now two others, both criminals,
were led away with him to be executed.

When they came to the place called the Skull,
they crucified him and the criminals there,
one on his right, the other on his left.
Then Jesus said,

✠ **"Father, forgive them, they know not what they do."**

N They divided his garments by casting lots.
The people stood by and watched;
the rulers, meanwhile, sneered at him and said,

C *"He saved others, let him save himself*
if he is the chosen one, the Christ of God."

N Even the soldiers jeered at him.
As they approached to offer him wine they called out,

C *"If you are King of the Jews, save yourself."*

N Above him there was an inscription that read,
"This is the King of the Jews."

Now one of the criminals hanging there reviled Jesus, saying,

V *"Are you not the Christ?*
Save yourself and us."

N The other, however, rebuking him, said in reply,

V *"Have you no fear of God,*
for you are subject to the same condemnation?
And indeed, we have been condemned justly,
for the sentence we received corresponds to our crimes,
but this man has done nothing criminal."

N Then he said,

V *"Jesus, remember me when you come into your kingdom."*

N He replied to him,

✠ **"Amen, I say to you,**
today you will be with me in Paradise."

N It was now about noon and darkness came over the whole land
until three in the afternoon
because of an eclipse of the sun.
Then the veil of the temple was torn down the middle.
Jesus cried out in a loud voice,

✠ **"Father, into your hands I commend my spirit";**

N and when he had said this he breathed his last.

Here all kneel and pause for a short time.

N The centurion who witnessed what had happened glorified God and said,

C *"This man was innocent beyond doubt."*

N When all the people who had gathered for this spectacle saw what had happened,
they returned home beating their breasts;
but all his acquaintances stood at a distance,
including the women who had followed him from Galilee
and saw these events.

The Gospel of the Lord.

GOOD FRIDAY, PASSION "A, B, C"

THE PASSION OF OUR LORD JESUS CHRIST ACCORDING TO JOHN 18:1—19:42

N The Passion of our Lord Jesus Christ according to John

N Jesus went out with his disciples across the Kidron valley
to where there was a garden,
into which he and his disciples entered.
Judas his betrayer also knew the place,
because Jesus had often met there with his disciples.
So Judas got a band of soldiers and guards
from the chief priests and the Pharisees
and went there with lanterns, torches, and weapons.
Jesus, knowing everything that was going to happen to him,
went out and said to them,

✠ **"Whom are you looking for?"**

N They answered him,

C *"Jesus the Nazorean."*

N He said to them,

✠ **"I AM."**

N Judas his betrayer was also with them.
When he said to them, "I AM, "
they turned away and fell to the ground.
So he again asked them,

✠ **"Whom are you looking for?"**

N They said,

C *"Jesus the Nazorean."*

N Jesus answered,

✠ **"I told you that I AM.**
So if you are looking for me, let these men go."

N This was to fulfill what he had said,
"I have not lost any of those you gave me."

Then Simon Peter, who had a sword, drew it,
struck the high priest's slave, and cut off his right ear.
The slave's name was Malchus.
Jesus said to Peter,

✠ **"Put your sword into its scabbard.**
Shall I not drink the cup that the Father gave me?"

N So the band of soldiers, the tribune, and the Jewish guards seized Jesus,
bound him, and brought him to Annas first.
He was the father-in-law of Caiaphas,
who was high priest that year.
It was Caiaphas who had counseled the Jews
that it was better that one man should die rather than the people.

Simon Peter and another disciple followed Jesus.
Now the other disciple was known to the high priest,
and he entered the courtyard of the high priest with Jesus.
But Peter stood at the gate outside.
So the other disciple, the acquaintance of the high priest,
went out and spoke to the gatekeeper and brought Peter in.
Then the maid who was the gatekeeper said to Peter,

C *"You are not one of this man's disciples, are you?"*

N He said,

V *"I am not."*

N Now the slaves and the guards were standing around a charcoal fire
that they had made, because it was cold,
and were warming themselves.
Peter was also standing there keeping warm.

The high priest questioned Jesus
about his disciples and about his doctrine.
Jesus answered him,

✠ **"I have spoken publicly to the world.**
I have always taught in a synagogue
or in the temple area where all the Jews gather,
and in secret I have said nothing. Why ask me?
Ask those who heard me what I said to them.
They know what I said."

N When he had said this,
one of the temple guards standing there struck Jesus and said,

V *"Is this the way you answer the high priest?"*

N Jesus answered him,

✠ **"If I have spoken wrongly, testify to the wrong;**
but if I have spoken rightly, why do you strike me?"

N Then Annas sent him bound to Caiaphas the high priest.

Now Simon Peter was standing there keeping warm.
And they said to him,

C *"You are not one of his disciples, are you?"*

N He denied it and said,

V *"I am not."*

N One of the slaves of the high priest,
a relative of the one whose ear Peter had cut off, said,

C *"Didn't I see you in the garden with him?"*

N Again Peter denied it.
And immediately the cock crowed.

Then they brought Jesus from Caiaphas to the praetorium.
It was morning.
And they themselves did not enter the praetorium,
in order not to be defiled so that they could eat the Passover.
So Pilate came out to them and said,

V *"What charge do you bring against this man?"*

N They answered and said to him,

C *"If he were not a criminal,*
we would not have handed him over to you."

N At this, Pilate said to them,

V *"Take him yourselves, and judge him according to your law."*

N The Jews answered him,

C *"We do not have the right to execute anyone,"*

N in order that the word of Jesus might be fulfilled
that he said indicating the kind of death he would die.

So Pilate went back into the praetorium
and summoned Jesus and said to him,

V *"Are you the King of the Jews?"*

N Jesus answered,

✠ **"Do you say this on your own**
or have others told you about me?"

N Pilate answered,

V *"I am not a Jew, am I?*
Your own nation and the chief priests handed you over to me.
What have you done?"

N Jesus answered,

✠ **"My kingdom does not belong to this world.**
If my kingdom did belong to this world,
my attendants would be fighting
to keep me from being handed over to the Jews.
But as it is, my kingdom is not here."

N So Pilate said to him,

V *"Then you are a king?"*

N Jesus answered,

✠ **"You say I am a king.**
For this I was born and for this I came into the world,
to testify to the truth.
Everyone who belongs to the truth listens to my voice."

N Pilate said to him,

V *"What is truth?"*

N When he had said this,
he again went out to the Jews and said to them,

V *"I find no guilt in him.*
But you have a custom that I release one prisoner to you at Passover.
Do you want me to release to you the King of the Jews?"

N They cried out again,

C *"Not this one but Barabbas!"*

N Now Barabbas was a revolutionary.

Then Pilate took Jesus and had him scourged.
And the soldiers wove a crown out of thorns and placed it on his head,
and clothed him in a purple cloak,
and they came to him and said,

C *"Hail, King of the Jews!"*

N And they struck him repeatedly.
Once more Pilate went out and said to them,

V *"Look, I am bringing him out to you,*
so that you may know that I find no guilt in him."

N So Jesus came out,
wearing the crown of thorns and the purple cloak.
And Pilate said to them,

V *"Behold, the man!"*

N When the chief priests and the guards saw him they cried out,

C *"Crucify him, crucify him!"*

N Pilate said to them,

V *"Take him yourselves and crucify him.*
I find no guilt in him."

N The Jews answered,

C *"We have a law, and according to that law he ought to die,*
because he made himself the Son of God."

N Now when Pilate heard this statement,
he became even more afraid,
and went back into the praetorium and said to Jesus,

V *"Where are you from?"*

N Jesus did not answer him.
So Pilate said to him,

V *"Do you not speak to me?*
Do you not know that I have power to release you
and I have power to crucify you?"

N Jesus answered him,

✠ **"You would have no power over me**
if it had not been given to you from above.
For this reason the one who handed me over to you
has the greater sin."

N Consequently, Pilate tried to release him; but the Jews cried out,

C *"If you release him, you are not a Friend of Caesar.*
Everyone who makes himself a king opposes Caesar."

N When Pilate heard these words he brought Jesus out
and seated him on the judge's bench
in the place called Stone Pavement, in Hebrew, Gabbatha.
It was preparation day for Passover, and it was about noon.
And he said to the Jews,

V *"Behold, your king!"*

N They cried out,

C *"Take him away, take him away! Crucify him!"*

N Pilate said to them,

V *"Shall I crucify your king?"*

N The chief priests answered,

C *"We have no king but Caesar."*

N Then he handed him over to them to be crucified.

So they took Jesus, and, carrying the cross himself,
he went out to what is called the Place of the Skull,
in Hebrew, Golgotha.
There they crucified him, and with him two others,
one on either side, with Jesus in the middle.
Pilate also had an inscription written and put on the cross.
It read, "Jesus the Nazorean, the King of the Jews."
Now many of the Jews read this inscription,
because the place where Jesus was crucified was near the city;
and it was written in Hebrew, Latin, and Greek.
So the chief priests of the Jews said to Pilate,

C *"Do not write 'The King of the Jews,'*
but that he said, 'I am the King of the Jews.' "

N Pilate answered,

V *"What I have written, I have written."*

N When the soldiers had crucified Jesus,
they took his clothes and divided them into four shares,
a share for each soldier.
They also took his tunic, but the tunic was seamless,
woven in one piece from the top down.
So they said to one another,

C *"Let's not tear it, but cast lots for it to see whose it will be,"*

N in order that the passage of Scripture might be fulfilled that says:
They divided my garments among them,
and for my vesture they cast lots.

This is what the soldiers did.
Standing by the cross of Jesus were his mother
and his mother's sister, Mary the wife of Clopas, and Mary of Magdala.
When Jesus saw his mother and the disciple there whom he loved
he said to his mother,

✠ **"Woman, behold, your son."**

N Then he said to the disciple,

✠ **"Behold, your mother."**

N And from that hour the disciple took her into his home.

After this, aware that everything was now finished,
in order that the Scripture might be fulfilled,
Jesus said,

✠ **"I thirst."**

N There was a vessel filled with common wine.
So they put a sponge soaked in wine on a sprig of hyssop
and put it up to his mouth.
When Jesus had taken the wine, he said,

✠ **"It is finished."**

N And bowing his head, he handed over the spirit.

Here all kneel and pause for a short time.

N Now since it was preparation day,
in order that the bodies might not remain on the cross on the sabbath,
for the sabbath day of that week was a solemn one,
the Jews asked Pilate that their legs be broken
and that they be taken down.
So the soldiers came and broke the legs of the first
and then of the other one who was crucified with Jesus.
But when they came to Jesus and saw that he was already dead,
they did not break his legs,
but one soldier thrust his lance into his side,
and immediately blood and water flowed out.
An eyewitness has testified, and his testimony is true;
he knows that he is speaking the truth,
so that you also may come to believe.
For this happened so that the Scripture passage might be fulfilled:
Not a bone of it will be broken.
And again another passage says:
They will look upon him whom they have pierced.

After this, Joseph of Arimathea,
secretly a disciple of Jesus for fear of the Jews,
asked Pilate if he could remove the body of Jesus.
And Pilate permitted it.
So he came and took his body.
Nicodemus, the one who had first come to him at night,
also came bringing a mixture of myrrh and aloes
weighing about one hundred pounds.

They took the body of Jesus
and bound it with burial cloths along with the spices,
according to the Jewish burial custom.
Now in the place where he had been crucified there was a garden,
and in the garden a new tomb, in which no one had yet been buried.
So they laid Jesus there because of the Jewish preparation day;
for the tomb was close by.

The Gospel of the Lord.